A Simple
CHRISTMAS SERIES
Presents

A 23-MINUTE MINI-MUSICAL ARRANGED ESPECIALLY
FOR UNISON AND TWO-PART CHOIRS

CREATED BY **MASON BROWN** AND **SUE C. SMITH**

COMPANION PRODUCTS:
CD Preview Pak 45757-2397-1
Listening CD 45757-2397-2
Split-Track Accompaniment CD 45757-2397-3
Split-Track Accompaniment DVD 45757-2397-6
Soprano/Alto Rehearsal Track CD 45757-2397-0
Tenor/Bass Rehearsal Track CD 45757-2397-5
Choral Book 45757-2397-7

www.brentwoodbenson.com

 a division of

© MMXIV Brentwood-Benson Music Publications, 101 Winners Circle, Brentwood, TN 37027.
All Rights Reserved. Unauthorized Duplication Prohibited.

CONTENTS

Emmanuel (Opening) 3

One King 12
   with God Rest Ye Merry, Gentlemen

Mary, Did You Know? 20

Silent Night! Holy Night! 28

Jesus Messiah 30
   with O Come, Let Us Adore Him

Emmanuel (Finale) 41

Emmanuel
(Opening)

Words and Music by
MARK HARRIS
Arranged by Marty Hamby

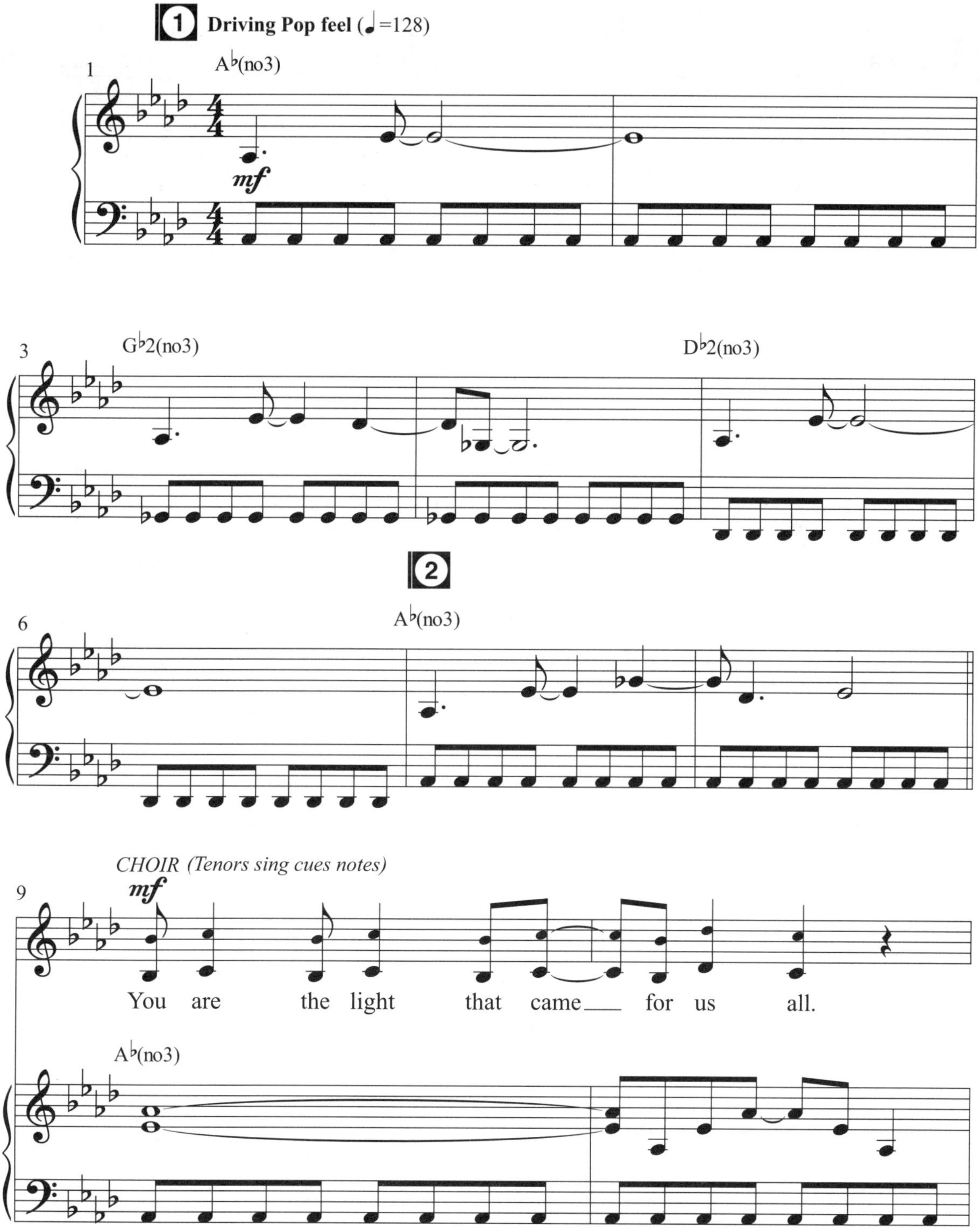

© Copyright 2008 New Spring Publishing / Ryanlynn Publishing (ASCAP)
(Administered at CapitolCMGPublishing.com). All rights reserved. Used by permission.
PLEASE NOTE: Copying of this music is NOT covered by the CCLI license. For CCLI information call 1-800-234-2446.

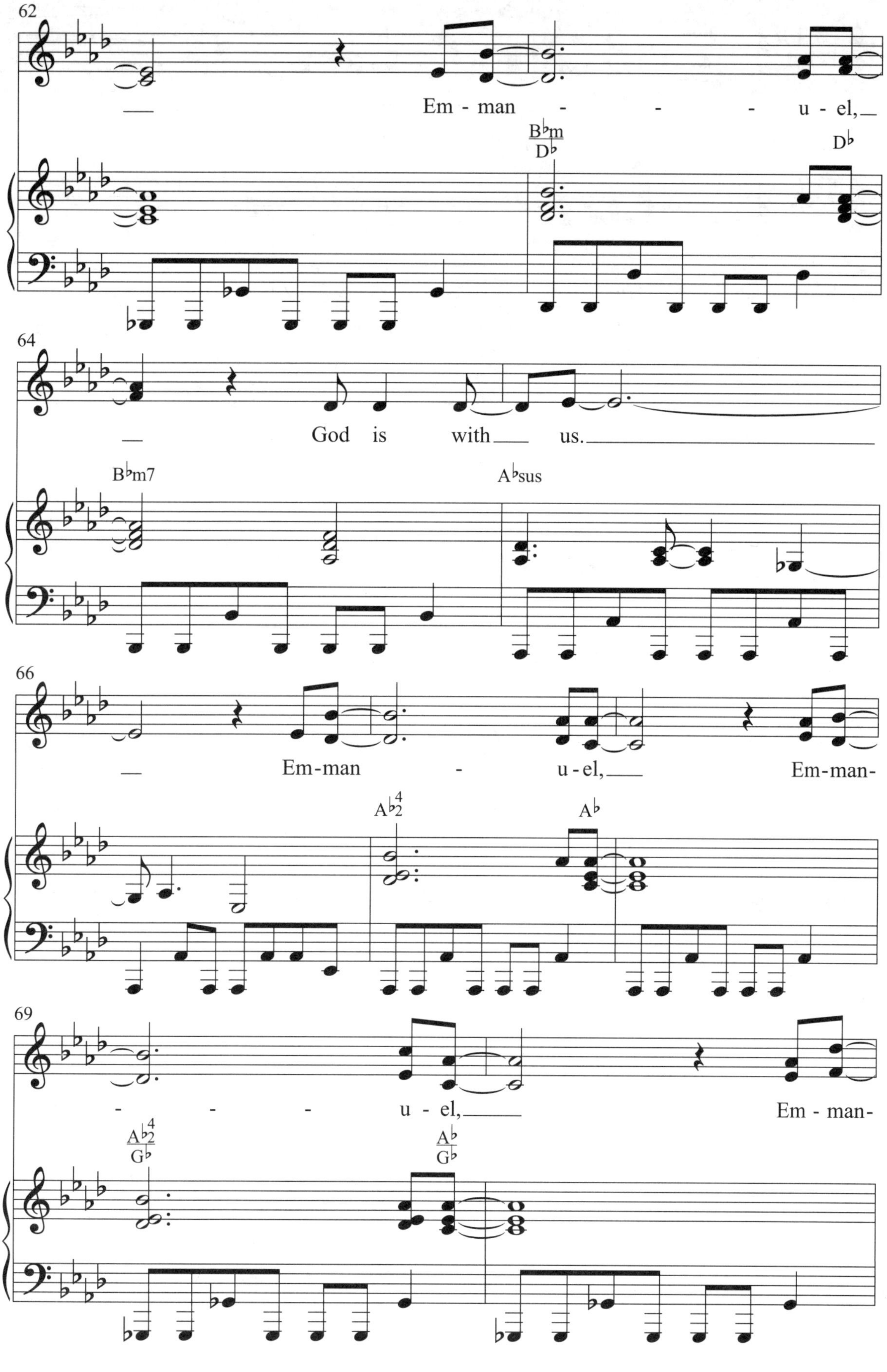
62
Em - man - - - u - el,
B♭m/D♭
D♭
64
God is with us.
B♭m7
A♭sus
66
Em-man - u - el, Em-man-
A♭4/2
A♭
69
- - - u - el, Em - man-
A♭4/2 / G♭
A♭/G♭

One King
with God Rest Ye Merry, Gentlemen

Words and Music by
JEFF BORDERS, GAYLA BORDERS
and LOWELL ALEXANDER
Arranged by Russell Mauldin

NARRATOR: Rejoice! A Savior has been born. God's Son has come to earth, and the world will never be the same. *(Music starts)* He is the One the prophet Isaiah spoke of when he said, "Behold, the virgin shall conceive and bear a Son, and shall call His name Immanuel." His coming was announced to shepherds, and at that same moment in a distant land, men of wealth and learning saw His star in the sky and would soon be on their way to find Him.

© Copyright 1998, 1999 (Arr. © Copyright 2014) Bridge Building Music / Randy Cox Music, Inc. (BMI)
(Administered at CapitolCMGPublishing.com) / Sony/ATV Music Publishing LLC / Grayson Castle Songs. All rights on behalf of Sony/ATV Music Publishing LLC / Grayson Castle Songs administered by Sony/ATV Publishing LLC (8 Music Square West, Nashville, TN 37203).
All rights reserved. International copyright secured. *Reprinted by permission of Hal Leonard Corporation.*
PLEASE NOTE: Copying of this music is NOT covered by the CCLI license. For CCLI information call 1-800-234-2446.

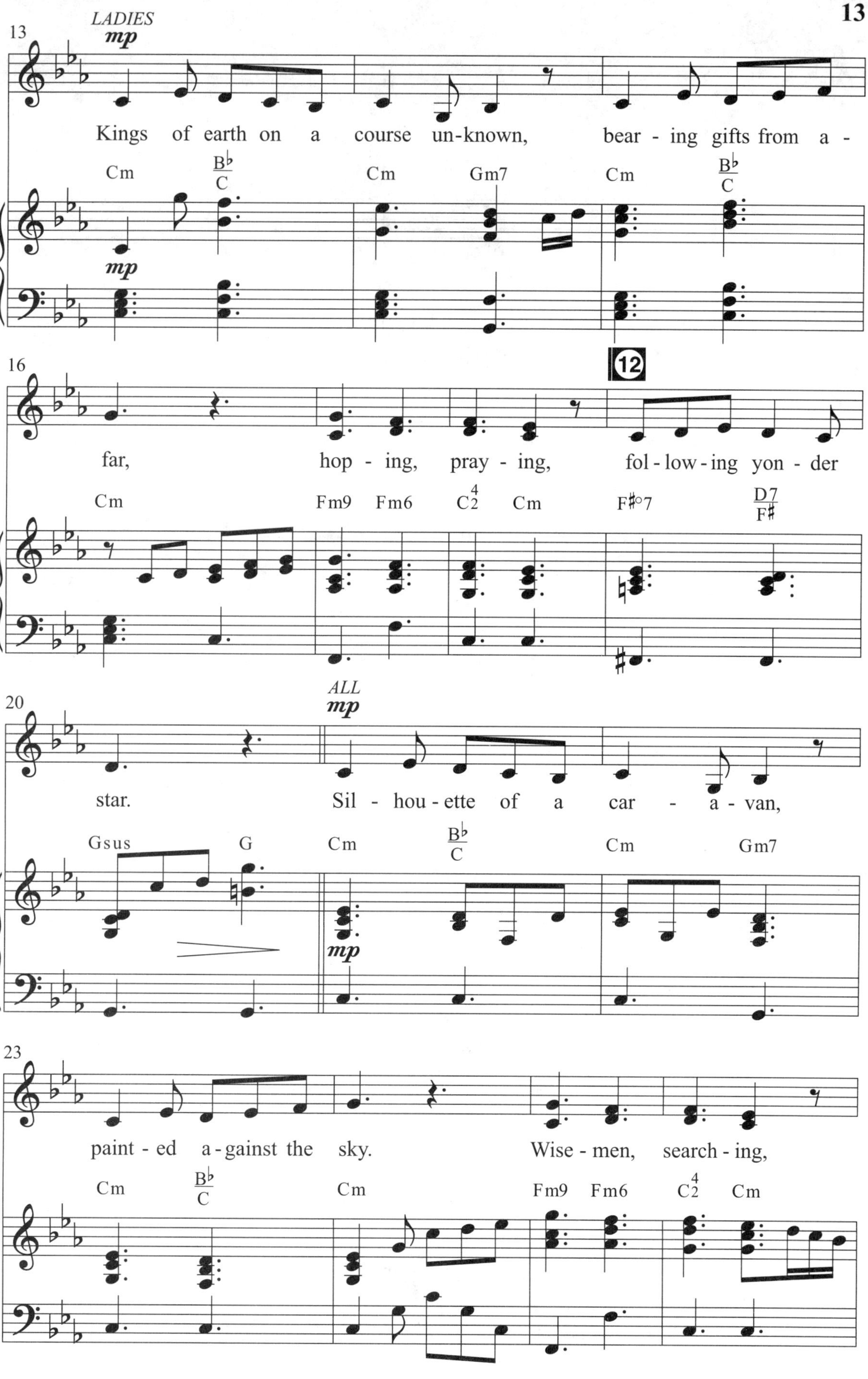
13
LADIES
mp
Kings of earth on a course un-known, bear - ing gifts from a -
Cm
B♭/C
Cm
Gm7
Cm
B♭/C
mp
16
12
far, hop - ing, pray - ing, fol - low - ing yon - der
Cm
Fm9
Fm6
C4/2
Cm
F♯°7
D7/F♯
20
ALL
mp
star. Sil - hou - ette of a car - a - van,
Gsus
G
Cm
B♭/C
Cm
Gm7
mp
23
paint - ed a - gainst the sky. Wise - men, search - ing,
Cm
B♭/C
Cm
Fm9
Fm6
C4/2
Cm

One king held the frank-in-cense. One king held the myrrh.

One king held the pur-est gold. One King held the

hope of the world. One King held the hope of the world,

the hope of the world.

Mary, Did You Know?

Words and Music by
MARK LOWRY and BUDDY GREENE
Arranged by Russell Mauldin

NARRATOR: *(Music starts)* The shepherds discovered the Savior just the way the angels had said they would — wrapped in swaddling clothes and lying in a manger. With the song of that heavenly host still ringing in their ears, they came in from the cold night, and fell to their knees before the Baby whose arrival the angels had celebrated. How was it possible, they must have asked themselves, that this Child was the Christ, the One who would save and deliver? Why was He here in this place where animals were kept instead of in a palace? Looking into the faces of Mary and Joseph, perhaps the shepherds saw that they had questions of their own. Yet this was not a night for getting answers, it was a night for faith. It was a night to gaze in reverent awe and simply imagine what God might have in store.

© Copyright 1991 Rufus Music (ASCAP) (Administered at CapitolCMGPublishing.com) /
Word Music, LLC. All rights reserved. Used by permission.
PLEASE NOTE: Copying of this music is NOT covered by the CCLI license. For CCLI information call 1-800-234-2446.

Silent Night! Holy Night!

Text by
JOSEF MOHR

Words and Music by
FRANZ GRÜBER
Arranged by Travis Cottrell

NARRATOR: *(Music starts)* Please join us in singing this beautiful song about our Savior's birth.

Arr. © Copyright 2010 Universal Music – Brentwood Benson Publishing
(Administered at CapitolCMGPublishing.com). All rights reserved. Used by permission.
PLEASE NOTE: Copying of this music is NOT covered by the CCLI license. For CCLI information call 1-800-234-2446.

Jesus Messiah
with O Come, Let Us Adore Him

Words and Music by
CHRIS TOMLIN, DANIEL CARSON,
ED CASH and JESSE REEVES
Arranged by Russell Mauldin

NARRATOR: *(Music starts)* That silent, holy night was just the beginning of the story of Jesus. Every step of His journey had been ordained. He had come to love the outcast, to care for the poor, to heal the sick, and to forgive sinners. Yet the true purpose for His life would only be realized when the road turned to Calvary and took Him to the cross.

© Copyright 2008 worshiptogether.com Songs / sixsteps Music / Vamos Publishing (ASCAP)
(Administered at CapitolCMGPublishing.com) / Wondrously Made Songs,
a division of Wondrous Worship & Llano Music, LLC (BMI) (Administered by Music Services). All rights reserved. Used by permission.
PLEASE NOTE: Copying of this music is NOT covered by the CCLI license. For CCLI information call 1-800-234-2446.

31

35

65
is in You. All the glo - ry to You,
C2 Dsus Am7(4)
68
40
God, the Light of the World.
G/B C2 Dsus
71
mf
O COME, LET US ADORE HIM (Traditional)
O come, let us a - dore Him! O
G D/G G Am/G G
mf
74
come, let us a - dore Him! O come, let us a -
D/G G C/E G/D D G/B Am7 G/B Am/C Em/C♯

41
77
dore___ Him– Christ_______ the Lord! For
D D/C G/B Am7 G/D D D7sus G
80
He a - lone is wor - thy! For He a - lone is
G D/G G Am/G G D/G G C/E
83
wor - thy! For He a - lone is wor - thy–__
G/D D G/B Am7 G/B Am/C Em/C♯ D D/C G/B Am7
42
86
mp
Christ_______ the Lord! Je - sus Mes - si -
G/D D D7sus G

- ah, name a-bove all names.

Bless-ed Re-deem - er, Im-man-u-el.

The res-cue for sin - ners.

The ran-som from heav - en.

40

Emmanuel
(Finale)

Words and Music by
MARK HARRIS
Arranged by Marty Hamby

NARRATOR: For every desperate heart, every soul in need of salvation, there is good news: *(Music starts)* God so loved the world that He sent His only begotten Son. Jesus has come and God is with us!

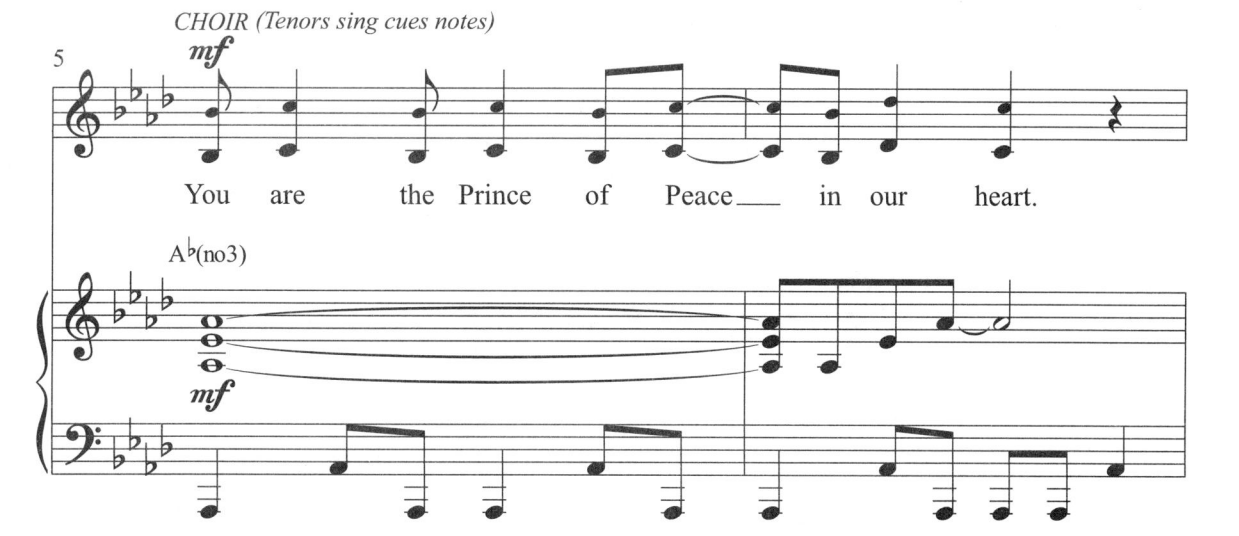

Driving Pop feel (♩=128)

CHOIR (Tenors sing cues notes)

You are the Prince of Peace in our heart.

© Copyright 2008 New Spring Publishing / Ryanlynn Publishing (ASCAP)
(Administered at CapitolCMGPublishing.com). All rights reserved. Used by permission.
PLEASE NOTE: Copying of this music is NOT covered by the CCLI license. For CCLI information call 1-800-234-2446.

You are the Way, the bright Morning Star. You are Em-man-u-el. You are the King we worship alone. All of the earth will bow at Your throne. You are

Em - man - u - el.

Em - man - u - el,

Em - man - u - el,

Em - man - u - el,

God is with us. Em-man-u-el, Em-man-u-el, Em-man-u-el, God is with us.

36
MEN
You're the light
for all
LADIES
You are,
E♭(no3)
38
to see.
for all,
all the world to see.
Fm7(4)
G♭2
40
You're the light
for all
You are,
E♭(no3)

42
to see.
for all,
all the world to see.
Fm7(4)
G♭2
44
You're the light
for all
You're the light
for all,
E♭(no3)
E♭
47
46
to see.
for all
to see.
Fm7(4)
G♭2

Subito mp
LADIES
Em - man - u - el, Em - man-
- - u - el, Em - man - u - el,
God is with us.
ALL
mf
Em - man-
- - u - el, Em - man - u - el,
A♭sus
A♭
A♭2 4 / G♭
A♭ / G♭
B♭m / D♭
B♭m7
A♭(no3)
mp

48

building

Em - man - u - el, ___ God is with ___ us. ___ Em-man - u - el, Em - man - u - el, ___ Em - man - u - el,

God is with us. Emmanuel, Emmanuel, Emmanuel, God is with us.

Em - man - u - el,
Em - man - u - el,
Em - man - u - el,
God is with us.

God is with us! God is with us!

Celebrate the reason for the season
with these Best-Selling Christmas Musicals from the

READY TO SING SERIES –
America's #1 Selling Church Choir Series

Arranged by RUSSELL MAULDIN

These musicals are perfect for the small to medium-sized choir, or the large choir with limited rehearsal time. Available in Easy SATB.

ORDER YOUR PREVIEW PAK TODAY!

The Ready To Sing Series available -
Exclusively through the **Brentwood Choral Club!**

Call **1-800-846-7664**, visit **www.brentwoodbenson.com** or order from your local Christian retailer today!